AF408380

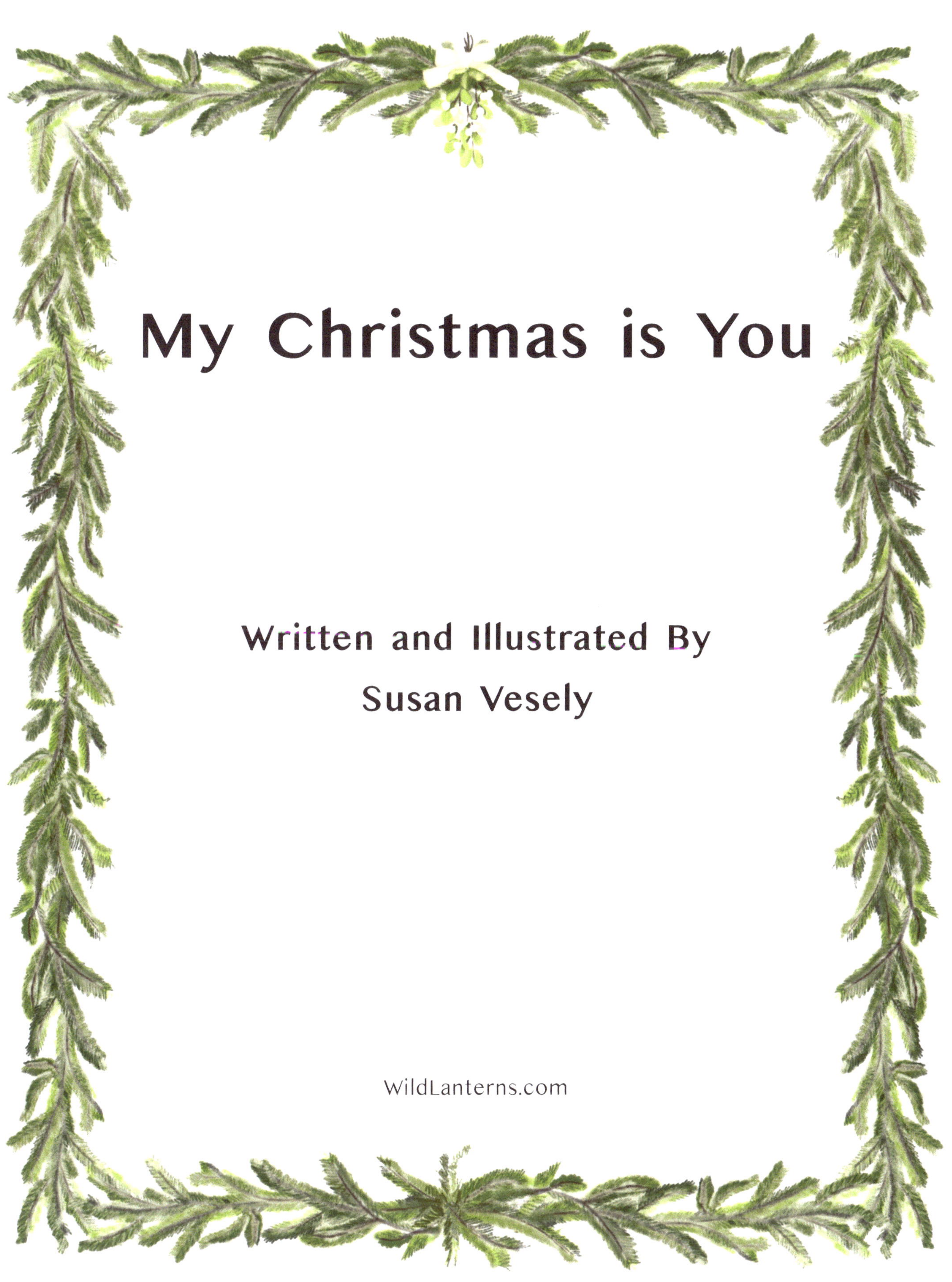

My Christmas is You

Written and Illustrated By

Susan Vesely

WildLanterns.com

For my family.

Dedicated to the people of Paradise, CA
and all who have suffered
loss from wildfires.

HOLLYWOOD

Today I set off for a much needed walk
I met with a friend to stroll and to talk
I told her my feelings were so discontent
And she patiently heard my sour lament

"It's 80 degrees, and, these stupid palm trees?!
Hollywood and Vine?
Give me snow drifts and pine!
The sun always shines, the leaves never fall
Let's face it, L.A. can't do Christmas at all!"

My friend chuckled, and sighed, and nodded her head
She thoughtfully considered all that I said.
She took a deep breath, knocked a stone from her shoe
As she straightened, she asked,
"What would Christmas look like for you?"

I stopped in my tracks,
I paused and I pondered.
And back thru the years
My mind started to
wander...

My Christmas appears the day after Thanksgiving

On a Friday that darkens the light way of living

Avoiding the stores that are oh so traumatic
We opt to pull boxes down from the attic

The cardboard is worn
and smells a bit musty,
But there's magic inside
(if not a bit dusty)

With garlands and bows
and lights that are tangled,
(We attempt to unravel
without getting strangled)

We festoon the eves, and deck out the halls
We frost window panes, and paste snowflakes on walls

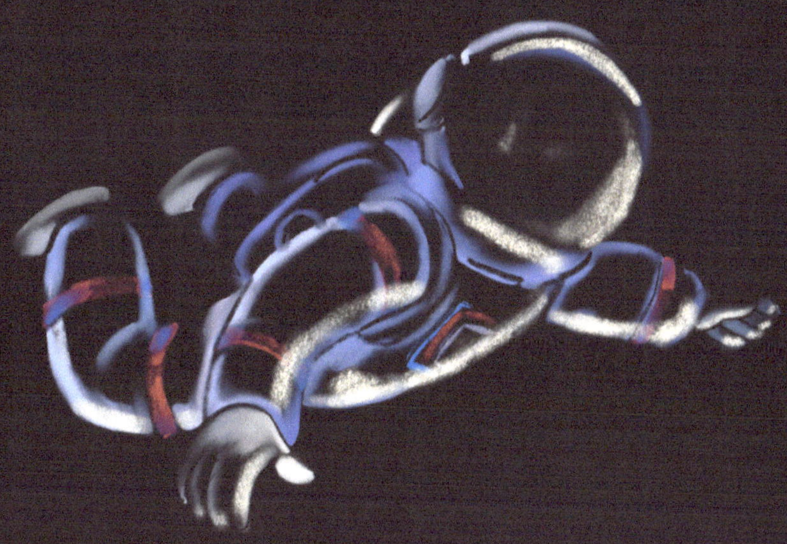

We hang lights from the roof, along sidewalks, on trees!
Our house is a place that even astronauts see

We listen to Frank and
Nat King Cole croon
And unpack enough baubles
to fill up the room

A real crystal bell,
And a goose that does tricks

A glittery frame made of
popsicle sticks
A cotton ball pom, and that
little glazed rabbit

Those vintage glass balls
that we keep out of habit

Each one is met with a memory of glee
And then carefully placed on our fragrant pine tree

Traditions are plenty, as are the treasures
Our family heirlooms have brought us much pleasure

The furry red stockings, each one to our name
With bespoke adornment, not one is the same

We go for long walks
in the frosty night air

And hand out baked goods
that are packaged with care

We slurp hot turkey soup alongside
fresh homemade bread

We sing carols, light candles,
and much more than I've said!

We watch Bing wish for snow
and Clark lose his head

Our Christmas is merry and jolly and bright
We celebrate family and brilliant star light
Coated with sentiment from the roof to the floor
Our Christmas, I think, doesn't need a thing more

BUT...

Then Something happened, and everything changed
A Monster rose up and became quite deranged
It stole all our stuff, it ate up our town
The home that I've known disappeared in the ground
And now our dear things will never be found.

Gone are the garlands and bangles and strings
Gone are the stockings and baubles that ring
Gone are the items so loaded with years
It seems like we're left with just ashes and tears.

"Christmas," I sobbed, "won't look like that again."

Then a thought crossed my mind and I started to grin

The memories are there as they were from the start
And the fire can't burn that Love out of our hearts

We can go for long walks and sing old Christmas songs
We will wrap gifts, cut snowflakes (our craft skills are strong)
We will bake like before, each tea cake and blossom
We can frost our own cookies (which is totally awesome)

And on Christmas Eve we'll still gather 'round candy
2 pounds worth! You'll see, it's going to be dandy

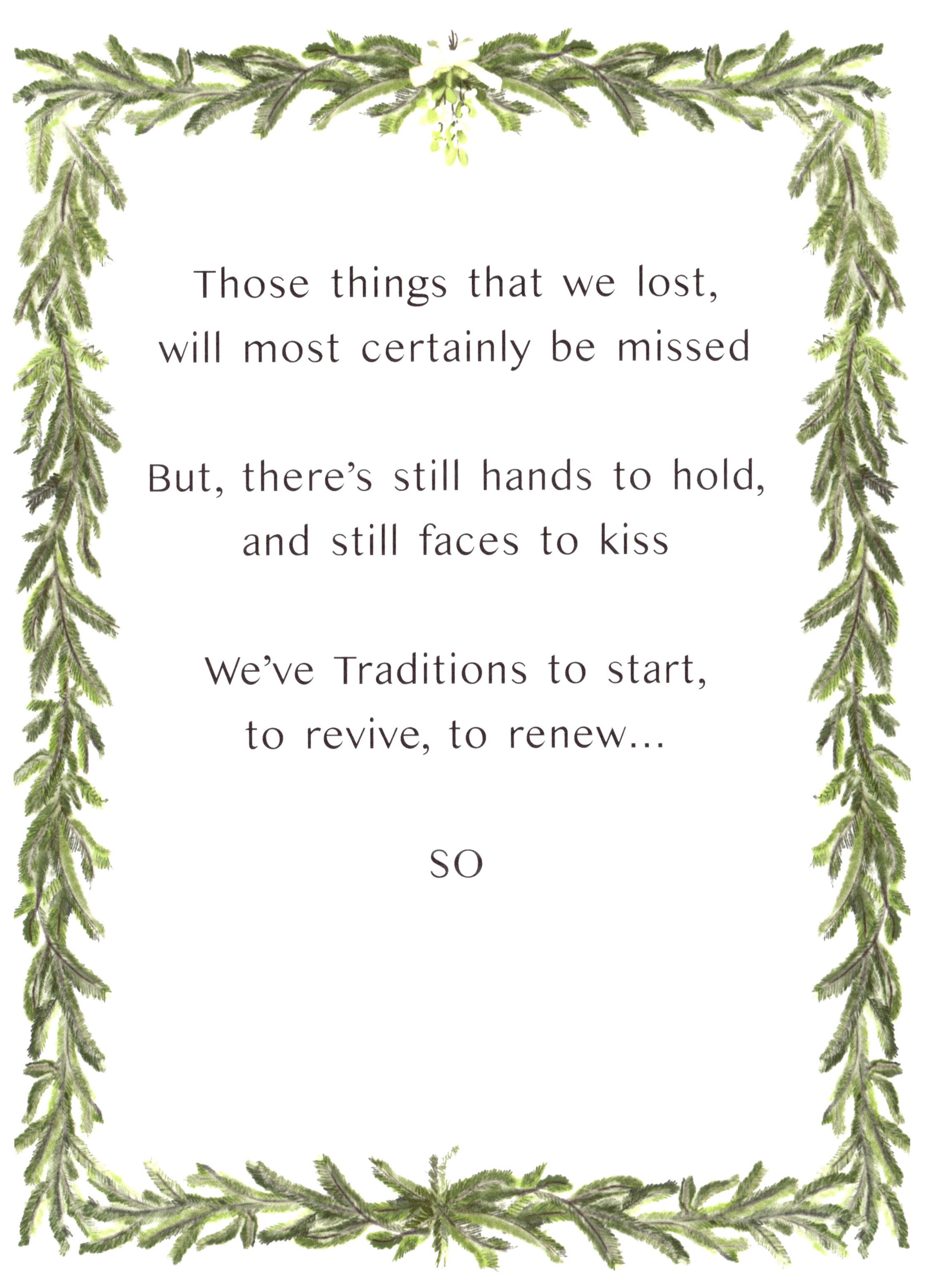

Those things that we lost,
will most certainly be missed

But, there's still hands to hold,
and still faces to kiss

We've Traditions to start,
to revive, to renew...

SO

I'm heading straight home

'cause, my Christmas is YOU!

www.ingramcontent.com/pod-product-compliance
Lightning Source LLC
Chambersburg PA
CBHW042028110726

48010CB00007B/273